I'm Not Really Forty

Male Edition

GW00691809

Jake Adie

jadie BOOKS

Published by
Jadie Books 2005

ISBN 0 9527082 6 4

Illustrations by Ian West

Typesetting by Jake Adie

Printed & bound by
Northstar Design
Colne
Lancs
BB8 9DB

Me Forty?

It's going to happen. I know it. I can just imagine the whole ghastly event unfolding before my eyes. The secret plans. The banners. The silly badges. The long lost friends with those stupid smiles. The cards. Oh no, the mobile discotheque. Please, please, please. I just know it. They're going to throw a surprise party for me. They think I'm going to be forty. Honest. But surely, if I can see what's happening why can't they? It's obvious that I'm not really going to be forty. I mean, I'm nothing like a forty-year-old. Never have been. Forty-year-olds are totally different to me. Yes, all right, I know, there are some likenesses.

We'll both have had a fair number of birthdays, for instance. Well, okay, if you want to be pedantic, forty. And I'll admit there's a reasonable chance that we've got kids who are growing up fast. Cheeky kids who think they know more than we do. Computer kids. Know nothing but computers. And we've probably both started to lose our waistline. And maybe our hair. But so what? You're going to have to do better than that to convince me I'm going to be forty.

Me. Them. We just don't relate to each other. We like different things. Have different values. We look different. Completely different. You know that. I know that. So why all the fuss? Why spend all that time and money celebrating? Even if I was about to turn into one of them I certainly wouldn't want to broadcast the fact. Shout it out from the rooftops that I'm going to spend the rest of my time on this planet as some sort of sad, secondary citizen. Someone so out of touch with reality that the closest he ever gets to being cool is when he does a couple of milligrams of fortifying substance from the local pharmacy before filling up his hot water bottle. I'm not stupid. I've been aware of the qualification requirements for ages. In fact, my dad used to be forty and he was nothing like me at all. He liked different music, clothes, cars, TV programmes (you know, documentaries and all that sort of stuff). And his attitude towards sex; well, ha, ha, ha, wait till you hear about that. You see, the act of spending forty-years as a human being and actually being an FYO have little to do with each other. They're poles apart. FYOs don't enjoy the same facility for constructive thought. They're intellectually inarticulate. Inept even. Way back when mankind was in its early developmental stages, their abilities to perceive ideas were established in such a primitive manner so as to render any future revision impossible. Carved in metaphorical stone so to speak. As if the component responsible for conceptual analysis was either waiting to be invented or had simply been left out. Or caught up on a back order maybe. Whatever, the mould was formed and there was no going

back. Enter
FYOs.
To be fair
though, there's
nothing to
indicate that
they weren't a
good idea at the
time. They must
have had their
uses and their
views,
inconceivably
limited though
they were, must
have performed
some sort of
effective social
function. Surely.
Otherwise why
would it have

seemed such a brilliant idea at the time? However, at the risk of appearing somewhat arrogant, I am just not prepared to be associated with their kind at this important juncture in my life. At this crossroads as it were. Not about to compromise my image and declare myself socially impotent just for the sake of it. Rid myself of the ability to play a meaningful role in the community. The nation. The world even. Like all other intellectually agile youngsters, I possess the ability to project my influence over vast areas of space. No trouble penetrating all manner of international barriers. In fact, when you think

about it, there's not much I can't do. If I want to, that is. If it suits me, you understand. All right, I'll explain. You may have guessed by now anyway but I'll, nevertheless, let you in on the secret; I'm on the net. Ehm, I am. The internet that is. Literally surf sites the world over. Cool or what?
There are

actually people

in the United States of America whose lives are just a little fuller. More informed. Worldly would be the right word I suppose. And all because of my visits. That's just one of the ways in which I choose to exert influence. Alter things for humble folk who may, one day, themselves, be unable to avoid FYO conversion.

My presence may just make all the difference. FYOs can't do that. Wouldn't know how to. Couldn't. They possess neither the technological acumen nor the equipment with which to make such monumental, history-in-the-making leaps. Sad, but true. They're just different. In every respect, right?

Take, for example, their approach to . . .

Clothes

Do we have to?
Yes, if you're
going to be
allowed access to
the mechanisms,
involved in this
society's
fascinating
ability to produce
an FYO-oblique-
non-FYO-rich
community
simultaneously
you're going to
need a bit more
evidence. If you
want to be
convinced that is.
Won't take long.
Quite amusing in
some ways. And

quite mind-boggling for most of us.

Trouble with FYOs is they approach fashion from a completely different perspective. Compared with us younger ones anyway. You see, rather than focus on the style or colour of a garment in order to achieve a pleasing visual effect, the FYO adopts a selection process that employs a wholly different set of criteria. For some inexplicable reason he ignores the logical paths followed by normal people and, instead, adopts a principle that would appear, to most of us, inappropriate in the extreme. Associating colour choice with shade of hair, design and cut with figure or general durability with intended usage bear absolutely no relationship to the considerations applied by our FYO. Whether or not the sartorial statement he inevitably makes compliments his character or stature is of absolutely no concern to him. No, our enigmatic FYO bases his purchase firmly on one consideration and one consideration only: size. Not size according to current trends or size dictated by the proportions of his frame. No, no, no. FYOs have just one fixed point of reference when restocking their wardrobe: their waist size — of twenty years ago. That's right, their midriff girth when they were just twenty years of age. I know, it's unbelievable.

A variety of suggestions have been put forward over the years in an effort to add a sort of sympathetic dimension to this curious tradition but one has yet to gain universal acceptance. BP (Belt Phobia) where the subject labours under the

Clothes

misapprehension that the act of exposing one's means of trouser fastening to all and sundry somehow reveals a deep subconscious need to rid the mind of some dark, childhood memory involving potties and safety pins has, in recent times, established itself as *the* consensus view amongst serious theorists.

25

But WADS
(Waistline
Accumulation
Denial
Syndrome),
which centres on
the Masochistic
Penance Theory
involving the
application of
undue pressure
to the stomach
region in a
symbolic attempt
to cast out the
devil who is
perceived to be
responsible for
his revolting,
gluttonous
habits, is

beginning to gain considerable ground.

To date, no effective antidote has been found and, until such time as it is, members of society are urged to exercise constraint if confronted by a sufferer and to avoid, at all costs, semi-concealed smirks or, worse still, open convulsive laughter with friends and associates at the expense of his somewhat obvious encumbrance. So, you see? — another example of my non-FYOness. All right, it would be a lie to suggest that my waist size relates closely to its former, youthful proportions but I could never be accused of having contracted BP or WADS. I'm not

even wearing a
trouser belt at
the moment. At
least, I don't
think I am. Hold
on a sec, let me
check. No, I don't
think so, wait a
minute, er,
what's this?
Ehm, er, no
that's not fair, I
mean it's not the
same thing. No,
I've just had a
rather large
meal, well, larger
than normal and
I'm about to take
a trip to the gym.
Yes, that's right,

I'm going to work out for half-an-hour. You know, pump some iron as us youngsters say. Well, I intend to. Providing they let me sign up as a member. Been meaning to do it for ages.
But it doesn't stop there. Consider for a moment FYOs' tastes in . . .

Music

You don't need to look a lot further than this to get a pretty good insight into what goes on in an FYO's head. Take a peep at what gets him groovin' (note cool apostrophe) and you've cracked it. Get through to the nucleus as it were. What makes him tick. And it's got absolutely nothing to do with an

appreciation of harmonic structures. Bears no relation. He doesn't give two hoots for the care the composer took to weave his soulful, stirring lyrics around an innovative, haunting melody line. Doesn't give it a second thought. Totally oblivious. No, all he's concerned with is the guy delivering the message. Not that he's into guys, don't get me wrong. No, all our FYO's limited powers of perception are able to focus on is the artist's ability to appeal to the chicks. The way he cavorts on stage. You might as well turn the sound down, it would make no difference. All that enters our friend's grey matter is the means by which his idol manages to lead a hoard of swooning, post-middle-aged females into some kind of simultaneous, mass-fakeasmic hysteria. Is that something you would want? But let us be honest with ourselves here, if such activity obliged one to assume the persona of Elvis Presley - the voice, the swagger and, in the saddest of cases, the white-and-gold-studded-turned-up-collar-suit, would it not place our basic ability to appreciate the arts firmly into question? Would it not? Wouldn't it occur to us that there may just be something missing in our whole view of the subject of music? Something slightly amiss? I tend to think so.

Don't you?
Yet another
example of my
obvious non-FYO
status. I shudder
even at the
thought of the
hip-wiggling old
codger. I
wouldn't want to
look like him if
you paid me a
million dollars.
Two million
dollars! Three
million . . .well . .
.anyway, you can
see where I'm
coming from. To
my, infinitely
more

sophisticated, cultured ear, music is one of life's most valued pleasures. Evocative, romantic, inspiring, uplifting, you name it, music can do it. Penetrates the soul. Stimulates the senses. Me, forty? Of course not. You know what I get off on? What's in my CD collection? Only the very latest cool dudes of course. Are you ready? Dire Straits, Fleetwood Mac, The Eagles - need I go on? It doesn't take a genius to see the difference. To acknowledge the fact that I could never be an FYO with up-to-the-minute tastes like these. There, I wasn't kidding, was I? But that's not all. Take the subject of. . .

Sex

I promised you this one, I know. And I'm beginning to regret having treated the matter with just a smidgen of mirth when I mentioned it previously. It really wasn't fair and I apologize to those who may have felt a little aggrieved. It isn't, after all, an FYO's fault to find himself lumbered with

such a catalogue of unfortunate approaches to life. And, of course, he can't be held singularly responsible for the gross indiscretions of his generation. If it was left to him, I'm quite sure the concept of wife-swapping would never have reared its ugly head. Never have occurred to him. He'd have just given up on the whole idea of sex as soon as he began to feel justifiably sympathetic towards his partner's sorry plight. How could she have been expected to anticipate the sudden metamorphic change in the one who swept her off her feet a couple of decades before? How could she have known? Might have been different if he'd come complete with an owner's handbook like most new acquisitions. Could've been a disaster though. You can just imagine how the section on routine maintenance might read: *"Although the topping-up of testosterone levels may not appear necessary, much of their effectiveness will have undergone serious degradation when the machine approaches the end of its useful life and it is recommended that the 'Prolongation Procedure' be put into practice at this time in order to maximize life expectation of the various component parts. Method involves firing up periodically on a*

*rotational basis
with owners of
similar models to
reduce general
wear and tear.
Any occasional
whines and
groans
emanating from
the region of the
head should be
considered quite
normal."*
Wife-swapping
does sound a lot
nicer I know, but
when it comes
down to it one
has to admit
there was little
need for the

exercise when
the machine was
first put into
service. And
considering
FYOs' short
shelf-life dates,
it's fair to
assume they
have little choice
in the matter.
Pity their poor
spouses, I say.
Or, put another
way, lucky old
me. Not on my
agenda to suffer
like those poor
souls. Still got
plenty of mileage
in my best-before

date. Oodles of it. Must have. Put it like this: nobody's ever presented me with an alternative front door key. Hasn't been necessary. In fact, come to think of it, my own one seems to have stopped working lately. Doesn't seem to fit properly. Been sleeping in the car these past few nights. Must get it fixed. Can't imagine why the wife hasn't missed me. Anyway, back to our unfortunate friends. Have you ever stopped to think about the way they behave while they're at . . .

Now, I appreciate you aren't in a position to make a valued judgement on my character. Wouldn't be easy without getting to know me. I realise that. So, for the purpose of this study, you'll have to accept the description I offer. However, you needn't worry in this regard because, as you've probably already

noticed, I'm a pretty modest, intelligent sort of fellow who's unlikely to get things wrong. Funny really, I've always been like that. My dear old mum, bless her soul, used to say that of me. Probably where I got it from.

Anyway, work. Me first. When I'm going about my daily routines I take great care and consideration to make sure that the boss gets his money's worth. Whether he's around to keep a check or not. Just the way I'm made. I've got enough savvy, you see, to realise that without due diligence on the part of a company's employees, there's little chance that there'll be any pay at the end of the month. You might, of course, manage to swing the lead for a while but, unless things are taken seriously and jobs are executed conscientiously most of the time, there really is no point in turning up at the damn place at all. Agree? Right. Simple, eh? Doesn't take a genius to get his head round that. And, as my guvnor will gladly testify, I've operated in this fashion ever since the first day I set foot on the premises. Still do it everyday. Whoops, nearly forgot; I also never have days off unless they're absolutely necessary. Bit of a gem really, even though I do say so myself. Now I'm prepared to accept, for the sake of this argument, that FYOs began their careers with a full set of like ideals firmly implanted in their heads. Fully intended to carry out their daily tasks with consummate integrity to both impress their new employer and warrant the prospects of future upward mobility. Had everything to play for. A young wife and family just round the corner maybe with the incumbent mortgage and household outgoings to consider. A significant step in one's life that can only be met by buckling down in the work place. No reason to think they got it wrong at that point.

But, in being fledgling FYOs rather than healthy young

men in the early developmental stages of their path to adult maturity, their attitude towards the whole matter of building a career soon became corrupted. By other, more senior FYOs no doubt. And the resultant effect on the remaining workforce was nothing if not disastrous. Their roles, as we are all fully aware, proceeded to be solely concerned with the evasion of responsibilities. In a devious, calculating manner: long lunches, fiddled expense accounts, pseudo business trips abroad (with company-funded condoms I wouldn't doubt), self-awarded bonuses, higher specification company cars, the list goes on and on. And all the time they're wallowing in this life of relaxation and debauchery, the real workers — the ones like you and me — are forced to slog away, often well into the evening, to support the buggers. And do they thank us? Do they remember us at Christmas? Do they heck? Not even a half-bottle of last month's Liebfraumilch.

Not even a glance in our direction. Why do we put up with them? And what do they get up to when they have some time off? When they get a chance to think about their . . .

Holidays

The average man spends something in the order of 30% of his time either travelling to, or being at, work. If you deduct the hours during which he is asleep you arrive at a non-work to work ratio of about 1:3 for the time he is awake. Conscious. Living. A long time by any standards don't you think? Put in a non-statistical

way, our working man finds it necessary to devote almost all of his life doing what he doesn't want to do in order to achieve a miserable few hours doing what he does. And this doesn't even take account of the time he devotes to getting ready for, and winding down from, work. Incredible eh? Some agenda. Who's wonderful idea was this?

So, it is no surprise that the odd weeks granted him by his employer as paid leave — weeks during which he may do as he pleases — should take on a sense of proportion, duration-wise, that bear little relation to any logical perspective. Every other fortnight comes and goes quicker than a change in the weather yet the prospect of a looming summer vacation will, quite rightly I suppose, present itself as some kind of interminable period away from the daily drudge. A kind of timeless opportunity to shake oneself free from the shackles of normality. Of course, in reality no such thing happens. But it is quite understandable that it should figure in the mind of the recipient so significantly. If not, what would life be worth? One isolated moment when we can fool ourselves into believing that we actually do work in order to live. So, what does our FYO do to maximize his impending euphoric state at the onset of his annual 336-hour-long sabbatical? When he is able to do just as he wishes. Anything at all. No limits apart from, maybe, the odd financial consideration. But even then he has almost infinite scope. Do virtually anything. Go anywhere. Right, where does he go? What does he do? Well, he goes to

Gatwick airport. That's right, London Gatwick. The one down the M23. He then makes a serious attempt to gain entry into the Guinness Book of Records by taking part in the *assembly-of-the-greatest-number-of-people-pushing-supermarket-type-trollies-full-of-suitcases* category. The event usually looks like a winner. Certain to warrant a mention in next year's edition. But for one reason or another it never does. The publisher's visiting adjudicator, no doubt, fails to get within shouting distance of the place and gives up. However, does that deter our throng of FYOs? Do they surrender their challenge and get on with the business of enjoying themselves? Not likely. They continue regardless. They shuffle, push, kick, shove, swear, curse, sneer, rant, rave, and make all sorts of other essential preparations for two-weeks in the sun. Well, not exactly two-weeks — after this ritualistic initiation ceremony, the statutory eight-hour flight delay and the reverse procedure when it's time to come home, it's more like 11-and-a-bit days. Of sheer unadulterated fun. Can you imagine? Moreover, can you picture a youngster like me opting for such a debacle? Wasting all those valuable hours? Getting all het up and angry when I should be relaxing? Can you heck! For the past five years I've made it my business to save religiously for a real holiday. One that will take me away from the hustle and bustle, the frustration and torment, the disorganization and confusion of a dedicated FYO-targeted, package nightmare. I'm going to whisk myself off to Florida. Orlando. Original, eh? I'll say. Going to do the whole Disney bit: Epcot Centre, Magic Kingdom, MGM. And Sea World probably. Universal Studios. Away from it all. Away from the crowds. Mixing exclusively with young folk like me. Plenty of time to think. Plenty of time to recharge the batteries before returning home in the right frame of mind to face another fifty weeks. Not exactly a typical FYO pursuit, eh? Well I told you so.

And, you know, FYOs can't even get it right when they are at home. Look, for instance, at one of life's most basic requirements. One that consumes vast chunks of our hard-earned income. *The basic life-sustaining constituent . . .*

Food

We do, after all, spend an awful lot of our time engaged in devouring the stuff, don't we? And the money it costs! Just think of the number of times we address the subject during the course of one day. Cup of tea in bed. Breakfast. Mid-morning chocolate snack. Coffee. Lunch. Afternoon tea. Dinner. Couple of pints. Cocoa.

That's nine separate participations. Nearly ten! Could be ten sometimes, perhaps. And there's a repeat performance the very next day. And the next. So, given the alarming regularity with which each of us voluntarily chooses to partake of these essential morsels, you would think it would follow that we would afford ourselves some kind of variety. You know, exercise a bit of imagination when drawing up the daily menu. Well, I'm pleased to report that most of us do just that. We scan the supermarket shelves for something a little different. Take time to tune into food and drink progs on the TV. Note what our friends, our work mates, are eating and drinking. Get an insight, even, into the delicacies partaken of in far-away lands. Alternative methods of cooking the stuff. And we feast our eyes on the features sections of the Sunday newspapers that dedicate themselves to the very subject and try to glean

something new,
or something
served, maybe, in
a different, more
imaginative
manner:
marinated with
sensuous oils and
juices, conserved
in exotic fruits,
enveloped in
succulent wafer-
thin pastry.
Makes me
hungry just
writing about it.
This is what *not*
being forty is all
about.
Yes, there is no
justification

today for allowing the palate to become bored. Tired of the same old calorific intake. Day after day, week after week. And it's not good for you. You just want to swallow the stuff as soon as it touches the lips. Don't you? Not good for the digestive system. Any doctor will tell you that. You need variety. Different flavours to stimulate the taste buds. It's the only way to ensure that each mouthful is adequately chewed. Savour the taste, reduce it to a consistency that will be welcomed by the processing equipment further down. More pleasure for you and fewer involuntary aural articulations to embarrass your friends. Makes sense, eh? But if, unlike me, you're unfortunate enough to be a pukka FYO, you won't see things this way. It won't even have entered your head. No, when you book a special table on a special occasion to entertain a special person in your life — when, more than anything else, you need to make an everlasting impression — something you'll both remember for years to come — an event that will be recounted to family and friends, colleagues and acquaintances well into the next decade; which culinary preference do you single out as the perfect accompaniment to the perfect celebration? Which one? Come on, own up. It's too late to backtrack now. Yes, it's none other than that perennial favourite, that all-time classic: chicken 'n chips. In a basket. The actual food, as you're probably aware, is somewhat immaterial, so long as it comes served up in a grease-stained, elongated wicker flowerpot. Accompanied by a paper serviette.

Beneath the food. What is it doing there? You can't exactly whip it out and drape it delicately across your lap, can you? And you can hardly use it to wipe around your mouth. You'd end up looking like a one-year-old after coming second in a confrontation with a quarter-pounder No, you just have to leave it precisely where it is, wait until it goes completely soggy, swallow the bits that have become permanently attached to the food and then wash it well down with a pint of lager. No option. Where did our FYOs come from? Is there any hope for them? Probably not. They don't even get it right when they're left alone with their . . .

Hobbies

Once a man has taken care to put his house in order: got himself a decent job, home, family maybe, car perhaps and other modern-day essentials: mobile phone, microwave, lawnmower, computer games, double-glazing etc., he can begin to consider how to fill those parts of his life which allow him to exercise real choice. Where he is free to develop areas of independence unhindered by the constraints placed upon him elsewhere. Financial constraints. Time constraints. Physical constraints. An opportunity to liberate himself for just a few hours each week. Choose what *he* wants. Indulge himself. Spoil himself. Do

something
outrageously
selfish. Every
man needs that,
don't you think?
Keeps him sane,
on the rails. Gets
things into
perspective.
Concentrates the
mind and
establishes an
identity.
Separates him
from the crowd.
And what better
choice of leisure
activities could a
chap have than
those available
to him in these

new millennium times? Everything you could imagine. Everything you *couldn't* imagine! No limits. Sports of all descriptions, music, concerts, theatre, cinema, books. Outdoor pursuits: rambling, mountain-biking, water-skiing, wet-biking, wind-surfing, land-surfing, *surf*-surfing, hang-gliding, microliting, grass-skiing, mountaineering, fell-walking, phew, tiring or what? But he can do these things. Any of them. *All* of them. Some of them. Whenever and wherever he wants. Doesn't have to cost a fortune either. Save up, do them — save up again, do them again. Simple, eh? So, can you give me one reason why our FYO hasn't stumbled across them? Any of them? One of them? Where is he at? He's only here once just like the rest of us. Time will run out one day. Doesn't *he* know that? Can't he see what is glaringly obvious to the rest of us? What is staring us straight in the face. Us *non-*FYOs. Clearly not.

Watch him on a Saturday

morning. Twenty-five past eight. Queuing up with the remainder of the town's FYOs waiting for the DIY store to open. Can't get in there fast enough. Doesn't have a clue what he wants. Just feels at home. Safe. Tell you what, let's follow him. Have a bit of fun. See what makes him tick. See if he *does* tick.

In he goes,
straight past
wallpapers,
ignores ceramic
tiles, wood
screws,
adhesives,
bathroom
displays, quick
glance,
gardening,
paints,
laminates, fitted
kitchens,
plumbing, still
no interest.
Lighting, wood-
fixings, picture
hooks, picture
frames, *pictures!*
Plywood,

fibreboard, plasterboard, plaster. Cement, sand, gravel. Where *is* he going? Hold on, he's lost. No he's not, he's looking for something. Turning round, few steps, shuffles to the right, on a bit further, left a bit, slower now, stops, begins to look a little on edge, anxious maybe, few beads of sweat. He's found what he's searching for. He's arrived at last. He's looking right at them. Not just in front of him but stretching out for miles to the left and right of him. It's twenty-three minutes to nine and he's the first FYO to arrive. Has the whole display to himself and the store isn't due to close for another nine-and-a-half hours. Sheer bliss. Pure unadulterated bliss. Two-hundred different power tools within inches of his trembling fingers. What he couldn't do if he had one of those. Total multi-speed, multifunction, dual-action, twin-headed control. He wants them all. Can't have them all. Maybe one. Two? But which two?

Let's leave him alone, he'll be there all morning. Have I made my point? Exposed the poor soul? Sad, eh? I've got to be off anyway. Too busy to hang around here. Got to get back and cut the grass. And the car needs washing and the windows have got to be, er . . . must go. Byeeee